CA$H IN ON
YOUR SKILLS

WAYS TO
MAKE MONEY WITH
COMPUTERS

JENNIFER LANDAU

Enslow Publishing
101 W. 23rd Street
Suite 240
New York, NY 10011
USA
enslow.com

Published in 2020 by Enslow Publishing, LLC
101 W. 23rd Street, Suite 240, New York, NY 10011

Library of Congress Cataloging-in-Publication Data

Names: Landau, Jennifer, author.
Title: Ways to make money with computers / Jennifer Landau.
Description: New York, NY : Enslow Publishing, 2020. | Series: Cash in on
  your skills | Includes bibliographical references and index. | Audience: Grades 7–12.
Identifiers: LCCN 2019013040| ISBN 9781978515468 (library bound) | ISBN
  9781978515451 (pbk.)
Subjects: LCSH: Computer industry—Vocational guidance—Juvenile literature.
Classification: LCC HD9696.C62 L357 2020 | DDC 331.702—dc23
LC record available at https://lccn.loc.gov/2019013040

Printed in China

To Our Readers: We have done our best to make sure all websites in this book were active and appropriate when we went to press. However, the author and the publisher have no control over and assume no liability for the material available on those websites or on any websites they may link to. Any comments or suggestions can be sent by email to customerservice@enslow.com.

Portions of this book originally appeared in *Money-Making Opportunities for Teens Who Are Computer Savvy* by Kathy Furgang.

CONTENTS

Introduction

According to a 2015 study by the Pew Research Center, 87 percent of teens between the ages of thirteen and seventeen have access to a laptop or desktop computer. Teens use computers to help with homework, stay in touch with friends and family, keep up with breaking news, and laugh at the latest memes.

Being computer literate is even cool now. In 2015, supermodel Karlie Kloss started an organization called Kode with Klossy to encourage teen girls to learn to code. The students learn programming languages like JavaScript, HTML, Swift, and CSS. Kloss began her work because she saw tech playing an important role in the fashion industry and wanted to show girls that they could incorporate programming languages into whatever field excited them, which would only make their skills more marketable going forward. Graduates of the program have created apps that track legislation in Congress, diagnose ADHD, and locate gender-neutral bathrooms.

It's important to have computer skills to keep pace with the modern world and workforce. It's also a great way to start making money as a teen while trying to figure out what you might want to study in college—if you choose to attend college at all. A teen who is skilled at web design, for example, can

Google is one of the largest tech companies in the world. The Android 8.0 Oreo statue, shown here, stands in front of Google headquarters in Mountain View, California.

help a local business or entrepreneur design a site that is attractive, puts content front and center, is easy to navigate, and works reliably. As someone just starting out, a teen would have to charge less than a seasoned pro, but he or she would learn invaluable lessons and start adding work experience to their résumé. Of course, the way to build up your client base using your computer skills—or in any business—is to do great work, keep your commitments, and treat everyone with the same level of respect you'd want to be treated with in return.

There are so many areas where a teen can excel, including tutoring someone online or in person, acting as a virtual assistant, designing an app, working at a store that sells computers and peripherals, or writing basic code. While using your computer to make money, you'll also learn lessons that apply to any field, such as the role that taxes play in business and the importance of accurate bookkeeping, although you'll need a trusted adult to help you with your finances.

Adults can also serve as mentors and can teach you skills such as programming languages or in-demand software like Photoshop, and also help you network with people who can help expand your business. A mentor can also help you learn so-called "soft" skills, such as communication, problem solving, flexibility, and time management. A mentor can give you a better sense of how to work in an office setting as you move past high school, whether as a solo contractor or part of an in-house team. By using your love of computers to earn money, you'll also get a clearer idea of the direction you want to take after high school and what degree or training you will need to begin a fulfilling career.

Turning Your Passion into Profit

I f you're a teen who loves all things tech and wants to make money while still attending high school, there are many options available to you. You can help clients set up—or tune up—their computers, offer lessons on software that will make them more productive, or show them social media sites that will make them feel like part of a larger community. You can also create your own website, which is a great way to advertise your services as a website designer for individuals or businesses. For those with a creative flair, designing a logo or helping to edit photographs might be an interesting path to take. And if you want to create an app, go for it! You'll sharpen your skills and learn a lot about what it takes to do well in business. The most important thing is to believe in yourself and your ability to achieve your dreams.

Become a Consultant

Some small business owners or citizens in your town may not have the skills and knowledge necessary to set up, update, or even operate their computer equipment. People may ask you all kinds of technology-related questions already, so why not offer your services as a consultant to these businesses or people for a fee?

A consultant works on a per-project basis, helping only when needed, and doing the job for a predetermined price. This kind of arrangement works well for both parties involved. The company can get computer tech services when it can't afford to hire a full-time, on-site computer technician, and the consultant gets the opportunity to use his or her skills to make extra money.

Even average people who hire consultants to work on a home computer would benefit from such a service. It often takes people a long time to learn the skills to set up or update a computer, especially if they are inexperienced with technology, or even a bit afraid that they will cause something to go wrong with the computer. They know it is better to hire someone knowledgeable and experienced to do the job in order to avoid inadvertently doing harm to their home computer systems through errors in procedure or other kinds of mistakes.

Working as a consultant is a great way to make money, gain experience, and offer services that can help others become better informed and feel less isolated.

Tech-savvy teens can have a flexible schedule that makes them available to their clients. They may need to troubleshoot when there is a problem. A client may not know what to do about a certain error message on the computer screen. The consultant who is available at odd hours and can project a calm presence can give that client peace of mind during a stressful time.

Teaching Others

Some of the very same people who might hire a consultant to help with their tech work may wish they could learn some of the skills themselves. Taking lessons from a skilled and knowledgeable tutor can help those who are inexperienced with, or intimidated by, computers and other digital gadgets ease themselves into the online world. It can help them learn Microsoft Word, Excel, PowerPoint, Outlook, or other programs that have left them feeling baffled.

Your clients might be older people who didn't grow up with computers like you did. They may not be as comfortable with just diving in and experimenting with new programs. Teaching them to feel comfortable with the basics—such as universal key commands for copy, cut, paste, and undo—can make them feel more confident. Showing them how to create new files, how to organize them in folders, and how to attach them to an email can make a world of difference. Sometimes all people need is someone who can work with them at their pace and answer their questions without being condescending. Offering one-on-one or small group tutoring classes might be all these people need to become accomplished computer users. You may help them gain both greater independence and social connectivity. Teaching people how to use video chat services such as Facetime, Skype, and Google Duo can keep them connected to family and friends across the globe.

As your students get more advanced, you can tailor the lessons to those things they really need or want to learn, such as social networking sites or complex design or accounting programs like QuickBooks. You can teach them all that you know about the programs, lead them through user guides and manuals, and direct them to user-friendly, online tutorials.

A Winning Website

Today, people rely heavily on the internet and the information it has to offer. If a new business in town does not have a website up and running when it opens, it risks losing business. If people can't look the business up at a moment's notice to find its hours, location, and other essential information, they may very well move on to the next competitor. But not every new company has the money to pay a large web marketing firm to design, operate, maintain, and update its website. A small business such as a

When creating a website for a small business, be up-front about what skills you can offer and what your work will cost. Also, choose a deadline date that is both fair and realistic.

lawyer's or a dentist's office may just need a simple website that you might be able to design and launch quite quickly.

You may already know how to do something like this if you have made personal websites for yourself or your friends or family members. If you are a real techie, you can certainly do the work from scratch and use a computer language such as HTML. However, there are great web hosting sites like WordPress or Wix that do much of the work for you. Using a free web hosting site will keep your costs down, and the client will be paying you as a middleman to do the website design work.

Remember that your clients are paying for your expertise so that they can spend their time focusing on what they do best—running their businesses. People with great design sense or up-to-the-minute computer skills can end up giving their clients a big boost. And the job—and income—doesn't have to stop there. Websites need to be updated regularly. Small businesses often do not have the time to do it themselves or the money to hire a full-time employee to do it. You may be able to include updating the site in your fee or work out separate, smaller fees for updating the site after it has launched. In addition to updating websites, companies may pay computer-savvy teens to update their blogs or maintain their social media accounts.

App Appeal

If you are full of original, inventive ideas, designing apps may be for you. Some of the most popular apps available were made by individuals working alone or with only one other person. There's a lot of money to be made in iPhone and Android apps. According to Fortune.com (www.fortune.com) in 2018, Apple paid app developers more than $34 billion. And there is no minimum age limit placed on those who submit apps for approval. Many of them have been made by

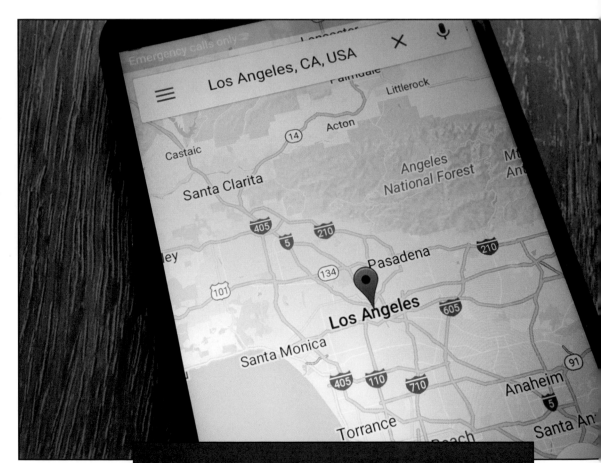

Major players like Google have a big advantage when creating apps like Google Maps. You can create an app as a teenager, but even a well-designed one may never catch on with consumers.

young people, some of them still in high school. But remember that there is fierce competition. Apple receives up to ten thousand submissions every week.

So how can a high school student get his or her app noticed in this vast sea of competition? First, you need a great idea. Then, once you know what kind of app you want to create, you need the skill to make it work correctly. Apple says that a vast majority of the apps it rejects are turned away simply because they do not work in some way. If you have a fun, technically sound product, you can begin to cross your fingers that it gets accepted. A good-looking app that is well-designed, fun, and easy to use—and has a practical, everyday utility—will increase its chances of being promoted and featured as a new app in the App Store.

However, making an app that is accepted and made widely available does not mean that you are guaranteed to make a lot of money. Many apps are free to download, and the ones that cost money won't necessarily be bought in great numbers. The important thing is to gain recognition as a talented app designer and continue to provide consistently creative, interesting, and useful apps to bolster your growing reputation.

You do not necessarily need much experience to develop a successful and popular app. Apple, for example, provides templates that let a designer automate payments or drop in images. Of course, whether that app will take off like Fortnite or Homescapes is anyone's guess. But creating an app will teach you the value of brainstorming, as well as perseverance, time management, and resiliency, all of which will serve you well in business and life.

Promote Yourself

You don't have to be a programmer or super techie to make money using your computer. Someone who is digitally literate can simply use the computer and internet to advertise other marketable skills he or she has to offer. You can use design programs such as Photoshop or InDesign to make posters or fliers to advertise your lawn-mowing service or availability as a dog walker. Try starting a Facebook page or using Instagram to promote your band's gig.

While you will not get paid for making your own promotional materials, you will save money that would otherwise go to a professional advertiser or designer. And, if you produce effective promotional materials, you will earn the money back by increasing the size of your client or customer base. If you were not computer savvy, you would be less effective in drumming up business for your dog walking or babysitting services.

A Talent for Photography

If you have a special knack for digital photography and computer-assisted image manipulation, storage, and sharing, you may want to think about earning money in that area. You can help people backup their photos using online sites like Apple's iCloud or Flickr, which offers not only a high quality photo stream but also a comments section similar to those on a social media site. You can also order photos from sites like Flickr and Shutterfly for albums and other keepsakes. Or you can perform some touch-up work with the help of a program like Photoshop Lightroom. These programs can easily correct poor exposures or image imperfections, crop images, or change color images to black and white. Navigating this ever-changing technology can be overwhelming so your guidance will be greatly appreciated.

Offering photo services can help you make money, and it can provide a good experience for someone who is interested in a career in the arts, photography, or design. People who want this service may be neighbors or family members who just returned from a big vacation with tons of digital images. Touching up and organizing and editing family photos can be a big help to people. Working with the family members to put together

Adobe Lightroom is photo editing software that allows users to organize and manipulate photos. There is a cloud-based version (Lightroom CC) and a desktop version (Lightroom Classic).

a digital photo album that can later be printed as a book is another possible business idea. Small businesses may benefit from your photo touch-up work as well if they are working on their own advertising projects.

A Creative Touch

Another idea for a computer-savvy teen with an artistic sensibility is to make designs on the computer and then have them printed onto T-shirts that can then be offered for sale. Using a program such as Adobe Illustrator can help you design logos or printed T-shirts for local organizations, sports teams, companies, corporate events, or charities. You can even design T-shirts for birthday parties, wedding parties and guests, or family reunion attendees.

The possibilities are endless for promoting special events, teams, or companies in your area. While many teams or events may use professional apparel companies for their promotional T-shirts and other garment needs, you may be able to generate some business from newer groups or organizations that may not yet have a large budget for such services. Using a vector-based program such as Adobe Illustrator will allow you to scale the images to the desired size to fit on any shirt or other piece of clothing upon which you wish to print. If you don't have the equipment necessary to print the T-shirts yourself, you can use a website that allows you to design a shirt online and then order the T-shirts to be printed and sent directly to you or your client.

If you're skilled at Adobe Illustrator, you can create designs and logos for a wide variety of products. Provide excellent service, and your customers will refer you to other businesses.

Marketing Your Work

Suppose you come up with a winning idea that you are very excited about. How can you let people know about the services that you will be offering? There are many ways to market yourself so that people know you are open for business.

FACEBOOK'S FOUNDER

Mark Zuckerberg was still in college when he founded the social networking site Facebook. And his interest in computers predated that. In the 1990s, he was a high school student and began writing software, learning Atari BASIC from his father and taking lessons from an experienced software developer.

By 2019, Zuckerberg was worth over $60 billion. But Zuckerberg's role as CEO of Facebook has not been without controversy. A voter-profiling firm called Cambridge Analytica obtained the Facebook

(continued on the next page)

Mark Zuckerberg is a very wealthy man but also a controversial one. There is widespread belief that under his leadership, Facebook has put profit above people's privacy and security.

(continued from the previous page)

profiles of more than fifty million users without their permission and later used that information in support of Donald Trump's 2016 presidential campaign. At first, Facebook minimized the effects of the leak but later agreed to take action. Facebook was also under pressure about Russian propaganda appearing on the social media site. This controversy has prompted increased discussion about the security issues that come with sharing information online.

The safest way for young people to start finding clients is to look to those people you already know. Make it clear to people you are close to that you are offering a particular service. Word of mouth through parents, friends, family members, and trustworthy acquaintances is a good way to find clients who are reliable and who will pay you for your services. Once you build up a good reputation with these clients, more will quickly follow through word-of-mouth recommendations and testimonials.

The Importance of a Professional Website

A website is a good way to advertise your services. It does not have to be anything elaborate. If you are advertising your own website design services, however, be sure that your own site's design is a good example of the work you will be able to do for your clients. Do a careful job and make sure all of your information is correct and any links to other sites are working correctly. When people see your attention to detail and your enthusiasm for the work you create, you should be able to win over some clients.

Expanding Your Résumé

Keep track of the things you have done that make you qualified to offer the services you are providing. A résumé is a list of your special skills and accomplishments. Each project you do for a client is something else to add to your résumé. As you continue to make money and build a base of clients, your résumé will become more impressive. You can hand out your latest résumé to new clients or update your former clients by letting them know how your business—and your skills and experience—have grown and evolved.

Your Portfolio Means Business

A portfolio is a visual display of your work. Portfolios may be in book form, but more likely they will be a digital collection put together on the computer. A digital portfolio can be saved on a flash drive or showcased on your own website or on a file hosting service like Dropbox. Showing clients a portfolio can help them to understand the type of work you do and the quality of that work. It is a great way to drum up new business and to clarify for clients what the end product might look like. It can convince clients that you are qualified to provide them with the digital services they need.

What's in Store?

Working as a solo contractor is not the only way to earn cash with your computer skills. Given the prevalence of computers, there are many jobs in stores, offices, and other workplaces where your expertise will make you stand out to a potential employer. Whether working after school, on the weekend, or during the summer, your ability to complete data entry tasks, help customers chose the correct computer, or teach software lessons at a local library can make all the difference in whether you are first on the list when it comes to being hired. Add in your enthusiasm and a willingness to pitch in with any task, and the job you want is within reach.

Selling Electronics

Someone who knows a lot about computers would be a logical choice for working as a computer and consumer electronics salesperson. Local electronics stores often hire young people during the summer and Christmas holiday seasons, as well as for weekend and after-school jobs.

Entry-level salespeople are given the basic information about the goods they are selling. But someone who understands the basics already—and perhaps knows far more than that—and who uses these kinds of products extensively at home and in school will be a valuable asset to his or her employer. It is helpful to understand computer terminology. It is also important to be able to explain complex technological concepts, capabilities, and utilities to customers who do not understand them or who are trying to decide on the best product to buy to suit their needs. Explaining the concepts and practical utility of processors, hard drives, screen resolutions, battery life, and task-specific software can be a daunting task for anyone. If you already understand something about processor speeds or which cables someone needs for peripheral equipment, customers will appreciate your insight and advice. They may even come back to talk to you again!

If you do choose this line of work, try not to sway the customer toward something that you might like for yourself. If you are partial to either a Mac or a PC, the customer should not be able to tell. Your biggest concern should be finding out how the person plans to use the computer. Then provide the customer with the computer that allows him or her to be a success, whether he or she

Working as a salesperson at an electronics store takes patience. Customers may be overwhelmed by the number of options and will need your guidance to choose what meets their needs.

is interested in complex design programs, online gaming, video editing, or simple word processing and spreadsheet applications.

A Variety of Stores

Have you ever been in a store and seen employees using scanners to look up inventory that might be stashed in the back storage rooms? More and more retailers are using computer technology to track goods and communicate with suppliers, their sister stores, and with customers. The people they hire to work in these stores will need a certain amount of computer expertise and training. People who understand the technologies and can even troubleshoot malfunctioning gadgets and computerized equipment could be an asset to the company and beat out fellow applicants for the job.

Teens with computer skills have an advantage over other job applicants. Even if the job is in retail, being able to use or fix scanners and other technology will make you stand out.

Explaining your technological abilities and interests while you are in an interview will help the employer see you in a different light.

The employer is dependent on technology and computers to keep many things in the company running, from the cash registers and the store's online shopping websites to its wedding and baby registries. Someone who is familiar with the technology and knows how to use it will have a big head start from day one. While every store has its own system, being tech savvy could cut down on the time needed to train an employee during busy store hours.

Working on a Database

Signing up at a temporary employment agency (or temp agency) for a summer position is a good way to find job opportunities that will harness your computer and digital skills. These agencies fill positions for companies that need help on short-term projects, often during the summers or around the holidays.

One of the most common temp jobs for teens is in the field of data entry. A company may need information entered into databases collected from customer satisfaction surveys, sales figures, or mailing list forms. Once the job is finished, the worker is no longer needed, so the work is considered temporary. Some of these jobs require training in special computer software, depending on what field the job is in, such as medicine or nonprofit organizations.

There are many opportunities for teens to make money online in data entry jobs. However, be very cautious of these opportunities. Many are scams that require money up front from you, and then no jobs come your way. Always get permission from your parents before starting any job, especially one that is offered online.

Your Local Library

Libraries today have computerized card catalogs. Working as a library assistant is a good way for teens to get experience with these computer databases. Once you get up to speed on the library's computerized system, you will be able to help people searching the library database to understand how the network searches work and how the card catalog system is organized.

In addition to the electronic card catalog systems at a library, there are also computer terminals available for the public to use. The people who use these terminals may not have a computer of their

You don't have to be a bookworm to work at a library. It's a great way to learn more about computer databases, and you might even get the chance to teach a class.

own, so they may not have the computer skills needed to search the internet or prepare files in word processing programs. Some libraries even offer computer training courses. You may be able to help assist and instruct these library patrons.

FINDING FREELANCE OPPORTUNITIES

For teens looking for freelance assignments as Photoshop editors, programmers, website designers, or other computer-related work, sites such as Fiverr (https:///www.fiverr.com) or Freelancer (https//:www .freelancer.com) might be a good fit. Both sites are free to join but take a commission from every job you book. Booking a job with these sites—or others such as goLance (https//www.golance.com) and Upwork (https://upwork.com) if you are at least eighteen— offer a chance to make money, improve your skills, and gain valuable experience that can lead to more advanced—and well-paying—contract work.

In order to attract clients, have a well-written profile, be clear about what skills you can offer, and always be professional. If you've done work for other clients, ask if they will provide testimonials. And always accept and provide work using whatever website you've signed up with rather than on your own. This keeps both you and the customer safe.

Working for a Local Business

Virtually all local businesses use computers, but if you can zero in on those companies that specialize in the design or manufacture of computer hardware or software, you may be able to get a great professional opportunity that would be unavailable to your less digitally literate peers.

For example, if there is a company in your town that makes microchips, getting a job there in any capacity can help you learn about the computer business. Even if you are working as an assistant, summer receptionist, or mailroom

Even if you're just fetching coffee at a computer company, you'll be exposed to innovative ideas and meet people who can help your career as you move forward.

33

clerk, you will have the opportunity to see how a real computer company works, what the atmosphere is like, if the work truly interests you, and if you have an aptitude for it. An added bonus is the opportunity to talk to some of the other employees and ask them questions about their jobs: how they got them, what they do at work, and if they like their position. This is where you can learn new things about the industry and what it takes to begin a career. You can also meet people who may be able to recommend you for other jobs in the future.

Applying Yourself

So where does someone who is interested in finding a job that might showcase her computer skills go? You can search websites like Indeed, ZipRecruiter, or Monster, or even the digital version of your local paper. The most important things are to be persistent and remain open to jobs that might not seem like the perfect fit at first glance. You never know where a position will lead or what brilliant idea you might come up with while you're on the job.

Always put your best foot forward. Most applications are online, but you may also be asked to fill out a paper application when you go in for an interview. No matter the format, talk about your skills in detail, using clear and concise language. While you don't want to brag, you do want to make sure that potential employers understand what makes you the ideal candidate for the job. The more you know about the business and what it does, the better you may be able to shape your experience and abilities to fit what the company is looking for. Always check the employer's website so you're aware of the company's priorities and culture.

When preparing for an interview, check out the company website to determine its vision, goals, and culture. The more you know about a business, the less nervous you'll be at the interview.

When you are called in for an interview, focus on discussing only those tasks that the job will entail. Don't steer the interviewer into talking about your computer skills if the job you applied for involves scooping ice cream or stocking shelves at a local convenience store. The computer skills should be an added bonus after the employer realizes that you would be able to adequately perform the job that was advertised.

The decisive difference between you and another qualified candidate for the job might be that you can help your boss fix the computer system if it crashes. Explain that you understand how computer networks function and that you could help update software or set things up so that the store can process purchases using Apple Pay or Google Pay. Play up your strengths, but remember to be honest about your abilities.

Getting Down to Business

When a teen sets out to make money using his or her computer skills, there is more to know than just how to create a website or teach a beginner the basics of Microsoft Office. Even a teen has to pay federal and, in most instances, state taxes. There are also labor laws relating to how many hours a teen can work, and while it's unlikely anyone will keep tabs on the hours an entrepreneur spends on a project, it is important to learn these laws to be viewed as a professional. It's also vital to learn how to network in order to find clients—and how to treat them well in order to thrive in the business world.

Understanding Taxes

Anyone who works for an employer, whether you are above the age of eighteen or below, must pay taxes. The federal government and most state governments require that a percentage of a person's pay go to them in the form of a tax. The taxes are used to help pay for government programs and services that keep the country in operation.

When you receive a check from an employer, taxes are already deducted from the amount you earned. If you have your own business, however, or if you are making money doing entrepreneurial work, you will have to report the earnings to the government yourself so that it is aware of your income. As a result, you will owe taxes on that earned income.

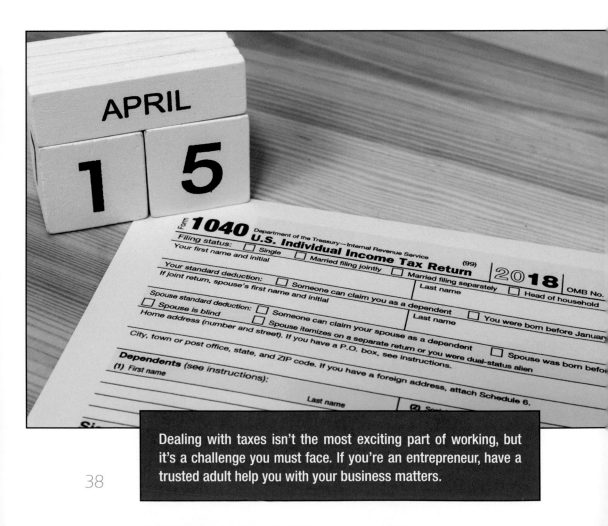

Dealing with taxes isn't the most exciting part of working, but it's a challenge you must face. If you're an entrepreneur, have a trusted adult help you with your business matters.

If you are engaged in any independent business ventures, be sure to have an adult help you handle your money and sort out your tax obligations. Some independent workers use an accountant to help them figure out what they owe in taxes. Others do it on their own using software such as TurboTax or H&R Block.

Some purchases you made to help you do your work—such as photo or video editing software—may be deductible from the amount of taxes that you owe. Make sure you are aware of the latest laws and regulations regarding how much people owe—including those who are self-employed—and what their possible deductions are. When in doubt, confer with a professional in this field.

Protecting Your Rights

The United States has labor laws that are designed to help protect the rights of workers. There are laws that set the minimum age at which teens are allowed to start working, as well as the number of hours that they are allowed to work per day and per week. If you are working for an employer at a store, library, or other business, he or she should be aware of the rules regarding how many hours you can be given as part of your schedule. However, if you are creating your own business in which you are paying other teens to help you, you must be aware of any restrictions your state may have.

If you are interested in entrepreneurship, it is imperative to learn as much as you can about the ins and outs of owning your own business. Labor laws are an important piece of the puzzle. For example, federal labor laws restrict minors under the age of sixteen from working during school hours, before 7 AM or after 7 PM, except during the summer, or more than forty hours a week during summers and holidays. While no one will likely check on you and enforce these rules, since you are not a certified business, it helps to know for the future what laws apply to teens. After finding out how old you must be to work in your state, you can apply for a work permit with your town. This will make you eligible to begin working for an employer.

The Social Network

Social networking platforms such as Facebook, Twitter, Instagram, Snapchat, and YouTube can help you promote a business or entrepreneurial idea without expending a lot of time and money. People with hundreds of friends on these platforms have the opportunity to get the word out quickly about their latest creations, services, and products.

Social media platforms can do more than connect you with friends and family. They are a great way to let people know what projects you're working on and that you are open for business!

You may wish to post a picture of an iPhone app you are working on or the design for a new T-shirt you are creating. You can let people know that your services are available as a tutor or technician. You can answer people's questions right on your timeline. Explain the kind of photo and video touch-up work or digital archiving services you can offer your clients. You can also create a YouTube video about all the skills you can offer or a collection of snaps called a Snapchat story. Word may spread to others, and you may get special requests. You may even end up with potential collaborators who you would never have imagined being able to work with otherwise.

A social networking platform is also a great place to get feedback about the work you have done. Clients might thank you online so that the praise is visible to all of your other friends and potential new customers. Positive feedback is great for drumming up more business and raising awareness about your skills, knowledge, and professional services. Your online presence can help people understand exactly how much you know about all things digital, which should be very good for business.

In fact, more than 60 million local business owners have created Facebook fan pages for their businesses. This is a good way to keep in contact with present and future customers and advertise to them directly. Even given the recent controversy surrounding Facebook's security breach, more than two billion people use the site worldwide. Starting a Facebook page to advertise your business ideas and services can help you reach many potential clients and, potentially, make a lot of money.

Making Face-to-Face Connections

Before the internet, there was face-to-face networking. If someone needed the help of a computer expert, he or she might ask friends, family, or coworkers for recommendations. Though there was no way to instantly connect with hundreds or thousands of people to get a message or request out quickly, traditional networking worked—and it still does. If you can connect with people and make a good impression on them, they will remember you the next time they need someone to help them.

Networking also involves making the most of your professional contacts. People you meet at work can be helpful to your career down the road. Suppose you work at a local business and you are interested in offering computer tutoring courses or computer technical assistance to people. Your boss, or anyone else you work with for that matter, can be a good source of information regarding potential new clients.

Networking works in many ways. Not only will people hear about you through word of mouth, but you will also get to hear about potential clients by keeping your ear to the ground and socializing with

Face-to-face networking may seem old-fashioned, but it is a great way to get to know people with similar interests, share information, and get connected with potential clients.

people of all ages. If you are interested in helping people understand their own computers or network their own businesses, ask your adult family members, family friends, and your friends' parents. They may know people who can use your assistance, or they may need it for themselves.

Keeping Customers Happy

Once you have found your clients, you must be sure to keep them satisfied. How can you do this? Offer services that they want, and provide them in a way that makes them happy. Customer service is a very important part of any business. It does not matter if you are working for yourself or if you are working at a big retail chain. Making a good impression and treating customers well are essential tools for building a good career, no matter what the field. Always wear professional attire when dealing with customers, and speak in a respectful, professional manner.

You may become frustrated with people who can't quite understand the difference between a computer file and a folder, and you may feel like speaking in a sharp tone or giving up altogether when they can't understand your directions for the tenth time. But be aware that your clients are paying you to help them learn because they thought you would be someone they could rely on to teach them in a way they would understand. If you become impatient and lose your cool, you won't be making a good impression, and you will likely not be asked to help the person again. You will also lose any chance of them recommending you to their friends and family.

If a customer is unhappy, that person will not use your services again. A smart entrepreneur would be available to answer any questions, troubleshoot, and calm a nervous client.

Customer service also involves getting back to clients in a timely manner when they contact you. When someone is having a computer problem, it could be an issue that needs to be taken care of quickly. If someone has lost files or needs help when a computer is acting up, you should be the calming and reassuring guide he or she so badly needs at such a stressful time.

WORKING AS A VIRTUAL ASSISTANT

Virtual assistants work remotely to provide a range of services to businesses. This could include scheduling meetings, marketing, design work, or website maintenance. If you work as a virtual assistant, you have to be flexible because you may have to take on last-minute projects and work for more than one business at a time. But it's a great way to gain experience and round out your résumé. You can look for work on job boards—make sure you meet the minimum age requirements—or by creating your own website and developing connections through clients you have worked for who can give you a strong recommendation. Although not a lot of teens use LinkedIn (www.linkedin.com), it offers a space where you can showcase your work and qualifications, and present yourself in a professional manner. You can also write posts about all things tech-related to show that you are knowledgeable about your field.

Ethical Business Practices

Another important part of making money is doing things the proper way. Ethics is a set of moral principles that guide a person's behavior. In other words, it means doing the right thing. In business, there is a set of unwritten rules about how to act professionally and behave properly with superiors, coworkers, people who work for you, and valued clients or customers.

When working in the world of computers, think about the ethics behind sharing software programs or files that are copyright protected. For instance, using copyrighted songs in a product that you will be selling is unethical—and illegal—because it is a form of stealing.

Another way to make sure that you are doing your best to be professional and honest is to make sure that the information on your résumé is accurate and that any samples in your portfolio are truly yours. If you worked on a project with a friend, make clear that you did not do the work completely on your own. Similarly, be honest in interviews and don't feel the need to sugarcoat your accomplishments to make it seem like you have more experience. This will only lead to embarrassment for you when you are asked to do something you aren't yet capable of doing. And whoever hired you will be disappointed by the gap between your claims of competency and your actual skill set.

Remember that people who have hands-on professional experience and marketable skills like yours at such a young age are rare. Relax and be yourself, and people will want to hire you for who you are and the specialized work that you can do.

Knowing What to Charge

One of the toughest questions to answer when offering any kind of business service is, "How much do I charge?" It's not easy to answer that question because each job will be different and each client will have different needs and varying budgets. You don't want to give them a number that is too high, or they may refuse the service. If you give a number that is too low, however, you are not earning what you should for the amount of work you are putting into the job.

Pricing your work correctly may take time and trial and error. First, think about whether other teens you know provide the same services you do, and try to find out the prices they charge. It is good to be competitive with your pricing, but your fees should fall within roughly the same range as peers who offer the same services.

When you consider what to charge for your services, think about any money you have to spend up front to get the work done. Did you need to buy any new software, cables, or flash drives to hold information? This cash outlay should be factored into the fee you charge. Make sure that the money you receive for the work will pay for anything you had to spend, while allowing you to make at least a small profit. The idea is to make money, not to spend money without being fairly compensated.

One reason that people may hire you to do computer work for them is that they assume a teen will not charge as much for the service because he or she is not as experienced as an older, working specialist. In addition, they know your operating expenses are far lower than those of a professional computer services, IT, programming, graphic design, or photo and editing company. Try searching online for what a reputable company might charge for the same service you are offering, whether it be technical support, computer classes, or photo retouching. Although you will likely have to charge less, don't undersell yourself if you do work at the same level as a professional.

Keep track of the hours that you have worked. Look up the minimum wage in your state to give you a good idea of the lowest amount that an employer would be required by law to pay you if you were on his or her staff. Then think about the skill level involved in what you are doing. Charge a higher price for work that requires more skill. Since you may very well be getting hired because you can do

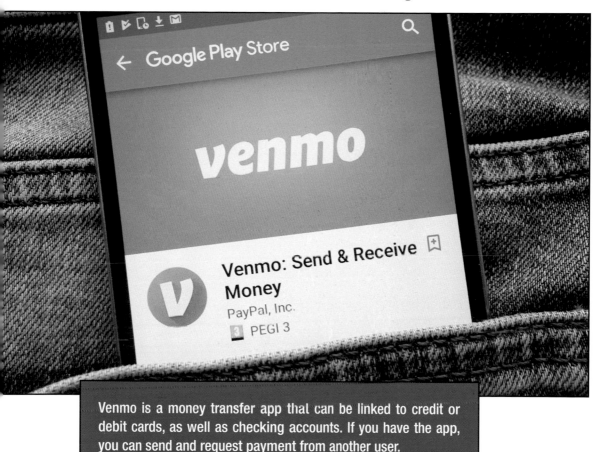

Venmo is a money transfer app that can be linked to credit or debit cards, as well as checking accounts. If you have the app, you can send and request payment from another user.

something that your client does not have the skills to do, be sure to increase your price a bit to reflect that. You will also be able to increase your prices as you gain more professional experience and add more jobs to your résumé.

It is important to decide with your client ahead of time how much you will be paid and the method of payment. Will you receive a check in the mail?

Will someone pay you through PayPal or give you cash? How long will the client have to pay you once the work is completed? It may be best to consult a parent or other responsible adult to get his or her advice on how you should accept payment for services rendered. And use a contract—often called a letter of agreement—so that everyone is on the same page about what services will be performed and at what price.

Investing in Your Future

Teens who have a talent for working with computers can take those skills and their entrepreneurial spirit and make money to spend on some long-desired object or experience—a new gaming system or concert tickets, perhaps—or to sock away for college. But your work can lead to more than cash. You can use what you've learned and the contacts you've made to carry that success far into the future. Even a volunteer position or internship, which may not put money in your pocket in the short run, can give you an idea of what career path appeals to you most, especially if you're given the chance to work in different departments within the company. Learning how to network, soaking up all the advice a mentor can offer, and proving yourself valuable to a team will help you build up not just your résumé, but your confidence, as well.

Part of a Larger Company

Working at a company that makes computer hardware, software, or digital related applications and accessories would seem like a dream job. These companies are not located in every town and community in the country, so consider yourself lucky if you have one near you.

Some companies provide state-of-the-art facilities that develop the latest computers. As an intern, you

If you're able to get a job as an intern at a large tech company, you will see how all the departments work together to create game-changing hardware and software.

might be exposed to the design department, hardware development, or the prototype development and testing departments. Keep in mind that some departments in a company may be working on confidential material that interns will not be allowed to be part of—or even see. However, you will still be able to learn a lot about how the company works, the products that are developed, and the range of jobs available.

Computer engineers work on developing computer systems and creating and analyzing software. To do this highly technical work, they rely on their advanced degrees in computer engineering. They must also stay on top of changes in the industry and be informed about their competitors' products. For example, cloud computing, which runs software or stores data over the internet, is now an integral part of any system.

Becoming an IT Star

Providing technical support to employees is a crucial job that IT departments perform. When employees need help learning new database systems or updating software, they call the IT department. When employees' computers crash, they lose important files or emails, or they are confused by a program they are working with, it is the IT department's job to solve the problem.

Sometimes training courses are developed by IT departments so that employees can learn how to use a new program, operating system, or database. The IT professionals have a wide range of knowledge of computers, networking, programming, and solving difficult problems related to hardware and software.

The work done by IT departments in big companies must be done on a smaller scale for community programs, nonprofit organizations, places of worship, and special events. These entities all use computers and digital information technology as part of their day-to-day operations or marketing efforts. Since many of these organizations have very small budgets, they would likely welcome your offer to volunteer your time, expertise, and digital-savvy computer services.

Volunteering is an important way to gain knowledge and experience and to see if you enjoy doing a certain aspect of computer work. If one of your friend's parents is starting a new business but does not have the money to hire someone to set up a computer network or write code for a simple database, you can offer a hand and see how the work suits you. That work experience will also look great on a résumé, which may lead to future work.

A MEANINGFUL MENTORSHIP

Having a chance to be an intern or volunteer at a company may result in your finding a professional mentor. Mentors are experts in their field who are willing to show you the ins and outs of a specific job. A mentor may be the supervisor of a department or someone who oversees your work on a particular computer-related project.

(continued on the next page)

Never take advantage of a mentor. Appreciate the wisdom and support he or she can offer, but remember that a mentor has other responsibilities besides helping you achieve your goals.

(continued from the previous page)

A good mentor will motivate you while also delivering honest feedback to help you grow both professionally and personally. By establishing this relationship, you will learn a lot about how to act in a workplace, such as how to ask questions of a supervisor while remaining respectful and how to take constructive criticism—an integral part of any job.

In return, as a mentee you should be mindful that a mentor is offering his or her time—with no pay—to help you expand your knowledge base. Acknowledge your mentor's generosity and work around his or her schedule. Also, put the suggestions you've received into action.

Training volunteers to learn a computer program for a special event is another good way to earn valuable experience. School computer labs often have student volunteers helping to maintain their networks and assist students who need help with computer basics. This kind of work can be rewarded with class credits or extra credit opportunities.

Although a volunteer or internship experience does not translate into money right away, it can be an important stepping-stone to great career opportunities. That's the most important part about

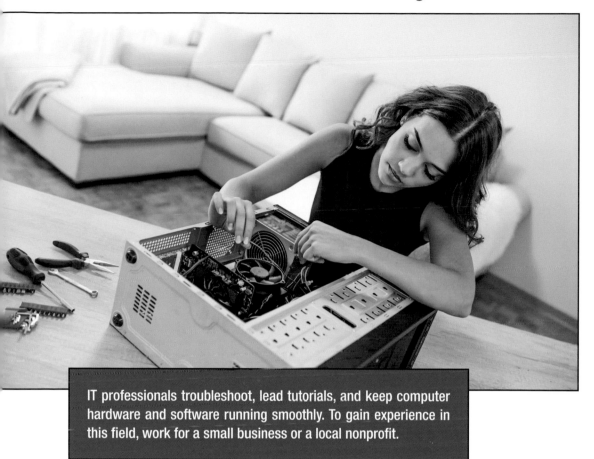

IT professionals troubleshoot, lead tutorials, and keep computer hardware and software running smoothly. To gain experience in this field, work for a small business or a local nonprofit.

getting into computer work as a teen. It is a building block for the future. Not only can it help you understand the structure of some companies and the work that computer experts do, but it also allows you to meet people who might be able to help your career after college, should you choose to attend.

Setting Career Goals

There are few fields that change as rapidly as computing. In order to stay competitive, whether working for yourself or for others, you need to stay current on both the technology and the culture. Luckily there are many ways to learn the newest trends: in classrooms, online, or even by using a manual by a reputable publisher. Another great way to share ideas is by joining a computer club, where you know you'll find like-minded teens eager to learn all they can. Keep up with your skills, and hold tight to your passion for computing. You're bound to be a success!

Always More to Learn

Learning about computers and digital technology is a job that's never done. There's always something new being developed that you will need to become familiar with. Computer classes are a good way to learn more and stay on top of the latest developments in the

Anyone who works with computers needs to stay current on changes in the field. There are many opportunities to learn, including classes at a community college and online tutorials.

field. There are great computer classes that are open to teens that can be taken at local community colleges and trade or technical schools, high schools, or even community centers. Websites like Lynda (https://www .lynda.com) or Udemy (https://www.udemy.com) offer a wide variety of courses. Neither site is free, but they may be available through your local library's website and often offer discounts or free trials.

Reading a print or online manual can help you learn the ins and outs of a computer, its hardware, its programs, and its operating systems. You can learn it simply for your own enjoyment or to become familiar with the finer points so that you can teach someone else how to master his or her computer system and its full capabilities.

Search your local library to see if it has computer manuals that can be checked out and read at home. Or look online to see if you can download an electronic version of the manual you want or to watch a tutorial about the program you wish to use.

A New Language

Computer programming is an extremely valuable skill to possess, and there are many computer languages that a person can learn. Machine language is the most elementary form of programming. This is a string of bits, or binary digits, of zeroes and ones. The 0 stands for no electric pulse, and 1 stands for an electric pulse. The string of electric signals in a certain configuration is the most basic language a computer can understand.

Assembly language is another low-level language that is a little easier to use than machine language, but it is also very limiting. It is tied to the hardware of a specific machine. At present, it is mostly used to fine-tune a particular program or write a certain type of process to ensure that it works as smoothly as possible.

High-level languages are specialized based on how they will be used. The purpose of high-level languages is to simplify programming. The term "high-level" comes from the fact that it is easier to understand and not designed for one specific machine or microchip. High-level programming

People who know how to code have a big advantage in the workforce. Learning high-level languages like JavaScript and Python will help you impress potential employers.

language is more like human language. Some popular high-level languages include JavaScript, which is used for web development, including web pages for sites such as Facebook and Gmail. Python is viewed as extremely user-friendly language with scientific and mathematical applications favored

CODING SUPERSTAR

Brittany Wenger calls coding her superpower, and few would argue with that view. When her cousin was diagnosed with breast cancer, Brittany set out to create an app that would advance cancer research. Cloud4Cancer is an artificial intelligence app that would diagnose whether breast cancer was malignant or benign with a 99.11 percent accuracy rate. Her app is now being tested in hospitals as a diagnostic tool that could prevent the need for invasive procedures, as well as reducing the price of diagnosis and treatment.

Brittany attributes her success to many factors, including her incredible work ethic and passion for improving cancer detection. Named to *Time* magazine's 30 under 30 list at nineteen, she has also given her own TED Talk, an event where prominent people speak about their area of expertise. With a plan to become a pediatric oncologist, Brittany has not only used her talent to gain a foothold in a prestigious field, but also to change countless lives.

by academics. Swift is popular for those building iOS applications, and C# for those who work with Microsoft platforms.

Staying on Top of Trends

Even the biggest computer moguls in the world have to keep up with the latest technological developments and newest consumer trends. Every

A virtual reality (VR) headseat, like the one shown here, is a device that allows the user to both see and interact with a simulated 3-D environment. The technology is currently changing and growing!

65

day new technologies are being developed and new products are being released. Keeping up with new tools and trends is crucial if you plan on having a career in computer and digital technology. If you do not keep learning about new technologies as a teen, your knowledge and expertise will quickly become outdated. By the time you graduate from college and set out on your career, you will—in technological time—be at least one generation behind.

Computer careers involve constant, lifelong learning. By the time you feel comfortable with a new program, an update or a new version is already available. If you are the type of person who embraces change and is an "early adopter" of new technologies and digital gadgets, you will thrive in the digital technology field. If you are teaching people how to use their computers or providing IT-style assistance to clients, it is essential to be up-to-date. This way you can do your job well and inform clients of new technologies that will help their businesses be as efficient as possible, satisfy and expand their customer base, and maintain a competitive edge. This will also open up new fields that may interest you going forward, such as robotics, digital gaming, virtual reality, or financial technology such as PayPal or Stripe.

Sharing a Common Interest

What better way to feel at home than by meeting up with like-minded people? If you are interested in starting your own business or making money with computers, join with other people who are interested in the same thing and form a club. Computer and entrepreneur clubs are a great place to connect with others who share your digital and money-making interests. Connecting with these people can help ideas flow, plans be realized, and goals met. You may even find a potential business partner!

Students who reside in Silicon Valley, in Palo Alto, California, live close to high-tech companies such as Apple, Hewlett-Packard, Intel, Google, and Adobe Systems. Students in this area have started clubs for entrepreneurs and tech savvy teens, spawning new apps and start-up companies. The clubs meet to discuss new ventures and ideas, and members talk about ways they can raise money to support their endeavors. They even have high-profile industry guests come in to speak about their experiences starting up companies and implementing their own computer projects.

A group like this can offer great opportunities to brainstorm ideas and develop projects and products. Whether your efforts make money now or down the

Tim Cook is the CEO of Apple. But whether you become as well-known as Cook, work for a small business, or consult, your computer skills will help you have a meaningful career.

road, you'll be thinking about the big picture when it comes to your career. But you don't have to go all the way to Silicon Valley to make a splash in the computer world. You can do that right in your own community. If you have the right ideas and the determination to make your mark in this field, you can climb the ladder of success all the way to the top.

GLOSSARY

app Short for "application," a computer program or software meant to fulfill a particular purpose.

artificial intelligence A field in computer science dedicated to building machines that can perform tasks normally reserved for humans.

assembly language A low-level programming language that is used in intercomputer communication.

binary A system of numerical communication, such as a string of zeroes and ones.

computer engineer A person who develops computer systems and analyzes software.

confidential Meant to be kept private or secret, for both personal and security reasons.

consultant A person who works on a project basis—rather than as a full-time employee—for a company.

database A structured set of data that is accessible by many people.

diagnose To determine the underlying cause of a problem by performing a series of tests.

Dropbox A cloud-based hosting service that allows both Mac and PC users to upload and securely store their files.

entrepreneur A person who develops, organizes, and operates a new business venture.

ethics Moral principles that govern the way a
person acts, including in business situations.

intern A student trainee who works, often without
pay, to gain experience in a given field.

IT department The information technology
department at a company, dealing with
systematizing, operating, and maintaining the
company's computer network and systems
and training employees to use company
computers, programs, and other relevant digital
technologies.

Java A high-level computer language that divides
objects into different orientations.

machine language The most elementary form
of programming, using strings of binary digits
to communicate.

manual A printed or digital set of instructions for
a particular topic of interest.

mentor An experienced and trusted adviser
who assists in one's academic and professional
education and advancement.

microchip Small chip that uses electronic signals
to tell devices what actions to perform.

minimum wage The minimum amount an
employer has to pay an employee, based on state
and local laws.

networking Developing or expanding business contacts in a respectful way to gain information and further your career.

Photoshop Software designed to edit digital photos using techniques such resizing, cropping, and color correction.

portfolio A physical or virtual archive of samples of a person's work that, when displayed, demonstrates that person's range, skill, and accomplishment in his or her field of endeavor.

programming The action or process of writing computer programs.

reputable Trustworthy; of good standing.

résumé A brief listing or summary of a person's education, professional experience, and qualifications for employment.

Silicon Valley The name given to an area of California that has a high concentration of computer and internet technology companies.

software Instructions that are tailored to make a certain program run on a computer.

temporary agency A service that fills a corporation's need for temporary employees with the right people who can perform the required job.

FURTHER READING

Books

Bly, Robert. *The Digital Marketing Handbook: A Step-by-Step Guide to Creating Websites That Sell.* Irvine, CA: Entrepreneur Press, 2018.

Bolles, Richard N. *What Color Is Your Parachute? 2019: A Practical Manual for Job-Hunters and Career-Changers.* Berkeley, CA: Ten Speed Press, 2018.

Chang, Emily. *Brotopia: Breaking Up the Boys' Club of Silicon Valley.* New York, NY: Portfolio, 2018.

Ferriss, Timothy. *Tribe of Mentors: Short Life Advice from the Best in the World.* New York, NY: Houghton Mifflin, Harcourt, 2017.

Penn, Maya. *You Got This! Unleash Your Awesomeness, Find Your Path, and Change Your World.* New York, NY: Gallery Books, 2016.

Schreier, Jason. *Blood, Sweat, and Pixels: The Triumphant, Turbulent Stories Behind How Video Games Are Made.* New York, NY: Harper Paperbacks, 2017.

Vaynerchuk, Gary. *Crushing It! How Great Entrepreneurs Build Their Business and Influence—And How You Can, Too.* New York, NY: Harper Business, 2018.

Wickre, Karen. *Taking the Work Out of Networking: An Introvert's Guide to Making Connections That Count.* New York, NY: Gallery Books, 2018.

Websites

www.kodewithklossy.com
The website of model Karlie Kloss's free 2-week
    coding boot camps for teenage girls.

www.fourhourworkweek.com
Business guru Tim Ferriss offers advice and insight
    into computing, career success, and how to live
    a balanced life.

www.codenewbie.org
This site offers Twitter chats, a blog, and podcasts
    for those new to coding.

BIBLIOGRAPHY

Adobe Photoshop. "Lightroom Killer Tips." Retrieved August 2012. http://lightroomkillertips.com.

Al-Heeti, Abrar. "Supermodel Karlie Kloss' Coding Camp Is Expanding." CNET.com. March 16, 2018. https://www.cnet.com/news/supermodel-karlie-kloss-coding-camp-for-girls-kode-with-klossy-is-expanding.

Baird, Leslie B. "Summer Jobs for Teens Working with Computers." Helium.com. July 22, 2010. http://www.helium.com/items/1900365-summer-jobs-for-teens-with-computer-skills.

The Beaker Life. "Stem Heroes: Brittany Wenger." Retrieved March 22, 2019. https://thebeakerlife.com/stem-heroes-brittany-wenger-9a41bb7ef594.

Bennington, Emily, and Skip Lineberg. *Effective Immediately: How to Fit In, Stand Out, and Move Up at Your First Real Job*. New York, NY: Ten Speed Press, 2010.

Berger, Lauren. *All Work, No Pay: Finding an Internship, Building Your Resume, Making Connections, and Gaining Job Experience*. Berkeley, CA: Ten Speed Press, 2012.

Berger, Rob. "8 Lucrative Business Ideas for High School Students." DoughRoller.com. Retrieved August 2012. http://www.doughroller.net/personal-finance/high-paying-jobs-for-high-school-students.

Berger, Sandra. *Ultimate Guide to Summer Opportunities for Teens: 200 Programs That Prepare You for College Success.* Waco, TX: Prufrock Press, 2007.

Boles, Blake. *Better Than College: How to Build a Successful Life Without a Four-Year Degree.* Springfield, OR: Tells Peak Press, 2012.

Campbell, Nicole. "Careers in the Computer Industry." eHow. Retrieved August 2012. http://www.ehow.com/about_5398557_careers -computer-industry.html.

Cheney, Alexandra. "Kid Entrepreneurs Build iPhone App." Inc.com. July 1, 2009. http://www .inc.com/news/articles/2009/07/iphone-app.html.

Doyle, Alison. "Work at Home Scams: Avoiding Job and Work at Home Scams." About.com. Retrieved August 2012. http://jobsearch .about.com/cs/workathomehelp/a/homescam .htm.

Ferguson Publishing Company. *Discovering Careers for Your Future: Environment.* New York, NY: Ferguson, 2008.

Fryer, Julie. *The Teen's Ultimate Guide to Making Money When You Can't Get a Job: 199 Ideas for Earning Cash on Your Own Terms.* Ocala, FL: Atlantic Publishing Group, 2012.

Gadara, Chirag. "Online Jobs for Teenagers—No Experience or Investment Required." GuideToEarnMoney.com. January 27, 2011. http://www.guidetoearnmoney.com/data -entry-jobs/online-jobs-for-teenagers-no -experience-or-investment-required-part-1.html.

Hardy, Quentin "Doing Apps and Start-Ups While Still in High School." *New York Times*, July 2, 2012. http://www.nytimes.com.

Hub Pages. "Types of Computer Languages with Their Advantages and Disadvantages." Retrieved August 2012. http://ninjacraze.hubpages.com /hub/Types-of-Computer-Languages-with -Advantages-and-Disadvantages.

Internships.com. "IT/Computer Technology Internships." Retrieved August 2012. http:// www.internships.com/intern/it.

Isaac, Mike, and Sheera Frankel. "Facebook Security Breach Exposes Accounts of 50 Million Users." *New York Times,* September 28, 2018.

James, Justin. "10 Things You Have to Know to Be Computer Literate." *Tech Republic*, February 6, 2012. http://www.techrepublic.com/blog /10things/10-things-you-have-to-know-to-be -computer-literate/3028.

Kelleher, Kevin. "Developer's $34 Billion Earnings from Apple's App Store Rose 28% in 2018."

Fortune.com. January 29, 2019. http://fortune
.com/2019/01/28/apple-app-store-developer-
earnings-2018.

Lagorio, Christine. "How to Make Money on iPhone
Apps." Inc.com. March 12, 2010. http://www.inc
.com/guides/making-money-iphone-apps.html.

Lehman, Jeff. *First Job—First Paycheck: How to Get
the Most Out of Both Without Help from Your
Parents.* Seattle, WA: Mentor Press, LLC, 2011.

Lenhart, Amanda. "A Majority of American Teens
Report Access to a Computer, Game Console,
Smartphone, and a Tablet." Pew Research Center.
April 9, 2015. https://www.pewinternet.org
/2015/04/09/a-majority-of-american-teens
-report-access-to-a-computer-game-console
-smartphone-and-a-tablet.

Mandell, Nancy R. "5 Summer Tax Tips for
Working Teens." Reuters Money. June 22, 2011.
http://blogs.reuters.com/reuters-money/2011
/06/22/5-summer-tax-tips-for-working-teens.

Misner, Ivan, et al. *Networking Like a Pro:
Turning Contacts into Connections.* Irvine, CA:
Entrepreneur Press, 2010.

Misner, Ivan, and Michelle R. Donovan. *The
29% Solution: 52 Weekly Networking Success
Strategies.* Austin, TX: Greenleaf Book Group
Press, 2008.

Swearingen, Jake. "Social Networking for Business." CBS Money Watch. September 5, 2008. http://www.cbsnews.com/8301-505125_162-51219914/social-networking-for-business.

Thelin, Nicole. "Labor Laws for Teens." eHow. Retrieved August 2012. http://www.ehow.com/about_5125665_labor-laws-teens.html.

U.S. Department of Labor. "Youth and Labor Age Requirements." Retrieved August 2012. http://www.dol.gov/dol/topic/youthlabor/agerequirements.htm.

Vohwinkle, Jeremy. "Jobs for Teens to Make Money." About.com. Retrieved August 2012. http://financialplan.about.com/od/students/a/Jobs-For-Teens-To-Make-Money.htm.

INDEX